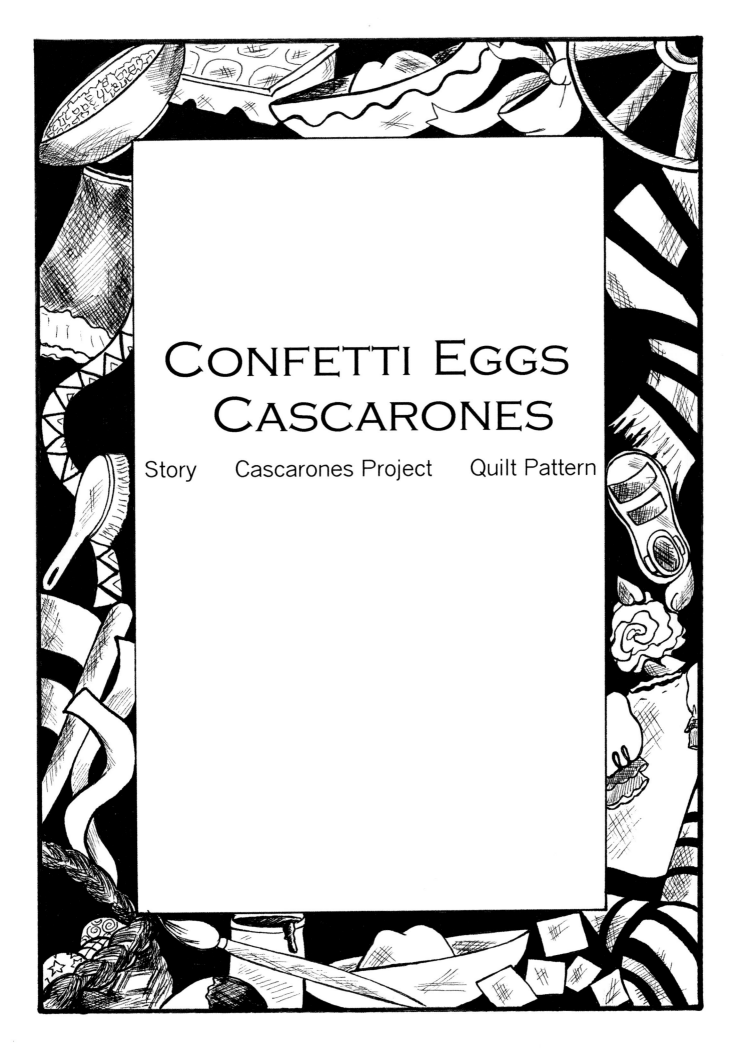

CONFETTI EGGS
CASCARONES

Story   Cascarones Project   Quilt Pattern

Confetti: Eggs / Cascarones
Copyright: 2001 Jane Tenorio-Coscarelli
Publisher: ¼ Inch Publishing
Copy Editor: Jane Tenorio-Coscarelli
Translation Editor: Nicole Coscarelli
Quilt Designer: Jane Tenorio-Coscarelli
Machine Quilting By: Homespun Quilting by Debbie Jenks
Quilt Photography By: Carina Woolrich Photography

Published By:
¼ Inch Publishing
33255 Stoneman Street #B
Lake Elsinore Ca. 92530 USA

Library of Congress Cataloging Card Number: 2001117634
Isbn: Hardcover 0-9653422-8-X
Isbn: Softcover 0-9653422-9-8

Printed in China
By Regent Publishing Services

10 9 8 7 6 5 4 3 2

To my sister Kathy the bravest person I know.

To the Baker Family for sharing
San Antonio and their Cascarones with me.

To my family and friends who have
supported me with words of encouragement.

For you the readers who have opened
your hearts to my books, while sharing
your treasured memories with me.

A heartfelt thank you,
Janie

"Nana, show me the way."

Note to the Reader

The purpose of our books is to introduce and expand Spanish vocabulary. We do not intend to teach the rules of Spanish grammar, sentence structure, or verb use. Therefore, all verbs that appear in the text are not conjugated in their proper form and are represented by their unconjugated, or infinitive form. We chose to keep verbs in their unconjugated form so that readers will become familiar with the root of the verb and be able to recognize other forms of the verb by identifying the root. Our hope is that by introducing Spanish vocabulary, readers will become interested in the Spanish language and will want to pursue learning the language on a higher level. We hope that you enjoy our stories and find them a valuable stepping stone to learning about another language and culture.

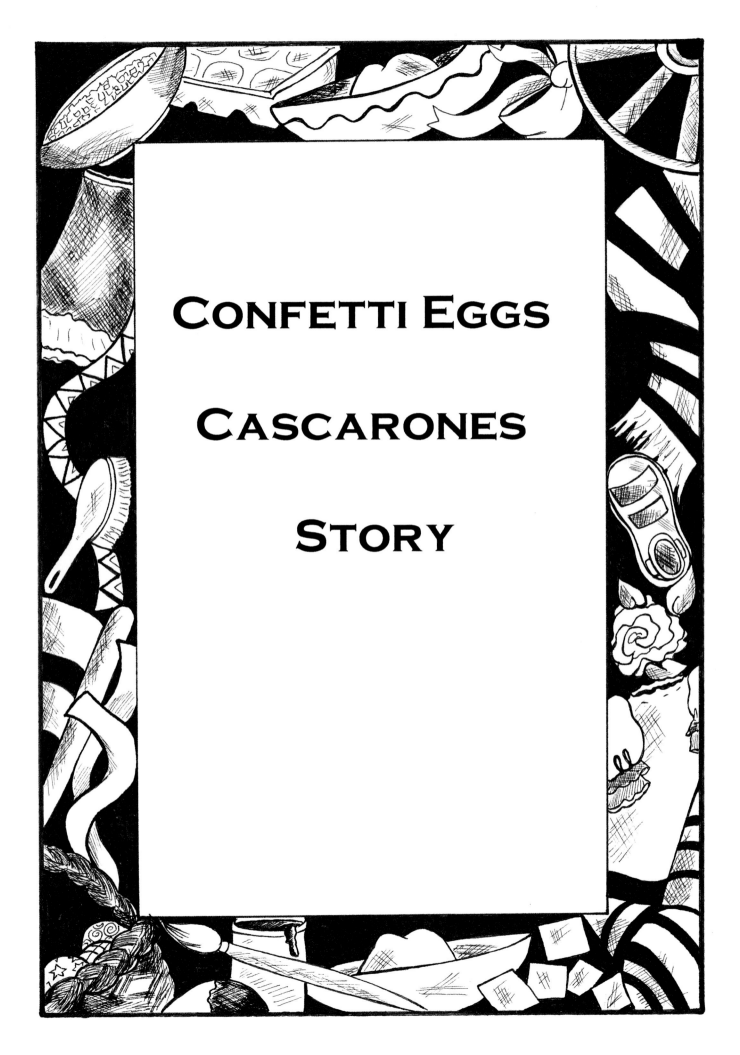

CONFETTI EGGS

CASCARONES

STORY

Angela stood at the kitchen **sink** while her mother braided her hair. As
lavabo
she turned her head, she saw a decorated **egg** sitting on the window sill.
huevo
"Mother, tell me the **story** of the confetti egg again, please," she asked
cuento
as she had so many times before. "Oh, Angela, I have told you that story

a thousand times," Mother replied. "Tell me again, please, **please**,"
por favor
Angela begged. "Okay, I will, but you must hold still so I can finish your

hair,"said Mother. Angela stood as still as she could and waited for her
pelo
mother **to begin**.
comenzar

When I was a little girl, I would **help** my grandmother make confetti
                              ayudar
eggs for the spring fiesta each year. Many weeks before the fiesta, we

started saving the egg **shells** from breakfast. When the fiesta grew
                    cascaras
nearer, we painted them bright colors, then we would stuff them full of

confetti and glue a tiny piece of paper over the top. We would fill a
confeti
basket with the confetti eggs and take them to the church fiesta. The
cesto
ladies of the **church** would sell them to raise money to buy school books.
              iglesia

9

Before one of the fiestas, Grandmother came and dressed me in my best

party **dress** and braided ribbons in my hair. Afterwards, she asked me if
    vestido
I could **deliver** the eggs to the fiesta by myself. My grandfather needed
     repartir
the **wagon** that day to work in the fields and she said the walk was too
    carro
far for an old woman like herself. She packed a **large** basket full of
                             grande
confetti eggs and wrapped her shawl around my shoulders. "Now be

careful my little one," she said as she kissed me good-bye. **"Bye**
cuidado   *Adíos*
grandmother! Bye," I called back as I walked down the road to **town.**
                                                      pueblo

It was a beautiful day. The **sun** was shining and the breeze felt good as it
sol
brushed against my cheeks. Soon the **road** beneath my feet became very
calle
rocky. My leather sandals caught in between the **stones.** I held on to the
piedras
basket tightly, balancing it as I stumbled down the road trying not

to break the beautiful eggs. Soon I made it a game, trying to step around
romper
each large stone, counting as I stepped. **"One. Two. Three,"** I
Uno. Dos. Tres
whispered. Before I knew it, the road became smoother.

The leaves from the trees danced across the road, reminding me of the

dancers I would see at the fiesta. Suddenly, a large barking dog came
bailarinas   *perro*
running towards me. My heart jumped and my feet froze in their steps. I

almost dropped the basket! I could see the dog's big, white teeth as he
                                                                dientes
growled at me. I took a deep breath. "Now dog, stop barking and be
                                                      gritando
nice," I said. "I am going into town for the fiesta to deliver these eggs for

my Grandmother, so please let me pass." I put my hand out so he could
      abuela
sniff it. His cold wet nose touched my hand as he sniffed. Soon he quit
                     nariz
growling and wagged his tail letting me pass after all.
                          cola

I could hear the **birds** in the trees singing their beautiful songs. As I
                    pajaros
walked a stranger approached me. He said, "Little girl, where are you

going with those **beautiful** confetti eggs?" "I am taking them to town for
                    bonitos
my grandmother, sir," I replied, not slowing down **to talk** to him. "Just a
                                                        hablar
minute, little girl, it is a long walk to town for a little girl like you. Why

not let me **buy** them from you? I will take them and **sell** them at the
            comprar   *vender*
fiesta. Then you can return to your grandmother. I have lots of money in

my pocket," he said reaching into his coat **pocket**." "No thank you, sir. I
                                            bolsillo
told my grandmother I would deliver them for her. Good day," I replied

as I began walking a little **faster** down the road towards town.
                            rápido

Soon I came to a small **bridge** in the road that crossed the stream.
puente
Walking up the bridge, I saw a red faced man working on his wagon.

"Excuse me, sir," I called from in front of the **wagon**. "Your wagon is
carro
blocking the road and I cannot pass." **"I am sorry,"** the man replied.
Lo siento
"The wheel on my wagon is broken and I must **fix** it so I can go on.
arreglar
Little girl, you will have to go down the side of the road and cross the

stream," he said pointing to the side of the road. "I am sorry, but that is
arroyo
the only way to pass."

I walked to the side of the bridge and carefully stepped down the side of

the **river bank**. The sand made me slip with each careful **step**. I stopped
    orilla   *paso*
at the stream's edge and looked for the shallowest place **to cross**. The
                                                        cruzar
water splashed on me as it rushed over the rocks. I took off my

grandmother's shawl and covered the eggs in the basket so they would

not get **wet**. I took off my sandals and stepped into the icy **water**,
    mojados   *agua*
carefully balancing my basket of confetti eggs as I slowly crossed. Once

across, I dried my **feet** with the shawl, put on my sandals, and continued
                    pies
on my journey.

I knew the journey was almost over when I could see the **roof tops** and
tejados
all the other people traveling towards town for the fiesta. Suddenly, I

heard someone calling my **name**. "Margarita! Margarita," called my
nombre
friend Johnny. He and some of my **classmates** were coming to the
compañeros
fiesta too. "Margarita, what do you have in your basket," Johnny asked.

"I have **eggs** I brought for the fiesta that my grandmother made," I
huevos
replied. "Oh, confetti eggs are so much **fun**," said Johnny. "Margarita,
divertido
why don't you let **us** all have some? Then we can break them on each
nosotros
other. Come on, egg **girl**." The others shouted, "Break them! Break
niña
them!" "No! No!" I shouted back, as I guarded my basket. "I must **take**
llevar
them to town." "You are no fun, Margarita!" Johnny yelled out. "Come

on, let's leave this egg girl and go to the fiesta **without** her." "Egg Girl!
sin
Egg Girl!" they all yelled as they **ran** towards town.
correr

More and more people began appearing on the road, many **laughing** and
riendo

talking. All of them were excited about the fiesta. Soon, I could hardly

 walk between everyone. "Pardon me!" I said as I tried to pass between
caminar

them. **"Pardon** me, pardon me!" I pushed my way through the crowd
 Perdóneme

toward the town **square**, holding my basket tightly and struggling to
 plaza

make my way through the crowd while trying not to drop or break the

beautiful eggs.

Finally, I reached the square where the **ladies** from the church were
mujeres
standing at their table. I walked up to the table carrying my basket of

eggs. **"Good morning,"** I greeted them. "Good morning," the ladies
Buenos días
replied. "Here are the confetti eggs my grandmother **made** for the
hacer
fiesta," I said as I placed them on the table. "Oh, how beautiful they are!

But **where** is your grandmother, little one,"one of the ladies asked. "She
dónde
is at home. My grandfather needed our wagon **today**, and the walk was
hoy
too far for her, so I brought them," I replied. "Oh, you are a **good**
buena
granddaughter to travel so far for your grandmother," said one lady as

she **counted** the eggs. "It was no trouble," I replied. "Please come sit
contar
with us,"they **offered**. "You will be able to see all of the fiesta from
ofrecer
here." "Thank you," I said, as I sat down.

I watched all of the dancers with their beautiful dresses of **lace**, and the
encaje

musicians with their shiny instruments. There were also funny **clowns**
payasos

with piñatas hanging from long wooden poles. The church ladies shared

sweet bread and candy with me. Soon people started coming to the table
pan dulce

and bought eggs from us. "Oh what beautiful eggs!" they said. "**My**
Mi

grandmother made them," I replied, smiling. Soon the basket was
abuela

empty making me a little sad. "We have raised a lot of money today for
vacio

school **books**, thanks to your grandmother's beautiful eggs,"one of the
libros

ladies said. "Yes, make sure to tell her **thank you**," another one added
gracias

as she handed me the empty basket. It was getting **late** and I knew I had
tarde

to start home before it was too dark to travel. "Good bye. Thank you," I

said to them as I started **walking** home.
caminando

When I opened the front **door** my grandmother was there to greet me.
puerta
"Mija, how was the fiesta? Did the eggs get there okay?" she asked.

"Yes," I replied and began to tell her **about** all the beautiful dancers,
sobre
 music, and piñatas I saw. I also told her that the ladies thanked her for
música
the beautiful eggs and that they let me sit with them and **shared** their
compartir
sweets with me at their table. I told her that all the people in the town

bought her beautiful eggs and when my basket was empty, it made me

a little **sad** to see them all gone.
triste

Grandmother smiled at me and held out an open **hand**. There in her
                                        mano
hand was an egg, the most **beautiful** confetti egg I had ever seen. "Oh,
                           bonito
grandmother, it is beautiful," I said. "For all your hard work and for the

long **journey** into town, I saved this one for you," Grandmother said as
     viaje
she handed me the egg. "Now you can break it like the other **children** in
                                                             niños
town do." "Oh no, grandmother! I am going to keep this one **forever**."
                                                           siempre
"But why, Mija?" asked grandmother. "Because you made it and trusted

me with your little egg **treasures**," I replied, never taking my eyes off
                         joyas
the egg.

"So, now my beautiful egg sits here on the **window sill**," Mother
alféizar
continued. "Each day I can look at the egg and remember my

grandmother and how she **trusted** a very small girl on a long journey
confiar en
into town." Angela **kissed** her mother when she finished the story as she
besar
did each time her mother told it. Now Angela's hair was all braided with

ribbons and she was dressed in her best party dress of ruffles and lace.
cintas
Angela and her mother filled their basket with eggs for the fiesta. Angela

smiled, remembering one little girl's journey with a basket of **little**
sonreir   *pequeños*
confetti eggs.

The End

Did you find me on each page?

Confetti Eggs Cascarones Project

Supplies
12 - Raw Eggs
Easter Egg Dye or Food Coloring
Color Markers or Crayons
Confetti Paper
Tissue paper
Glue stick or paste
(Parental supervision recommended)

Photo courtesy of the Baker Family

1. Hold egg over a large bowl to catch yoke and egg white. Save empty egg carton for later use.
2. Cut a quarter size hole at top of egg (pointed end) using a sharp knife.
3. Hold egg over bowl. Using a sharp pin make a tiny hole at other end. Egg white and yoke should pour out into bowl easily.
4. Repeat until a dozen have been emptied. Save yokes and whites for your morning breakfast. Refrigerate until needed.
5. Rinse egg shells with water until clean.
6. Place on a cookie sheet lined with paper towels to dry with open side down.
7. If using egg dye, mix according to instruction on box.
   If using food coloring, drop a few drops into a small cup or bowl of warm water. Stir.
8. Dip dry egg shell into colored water or dye. Let dry with open side down.
9. Stuff each dry egg with confetti about ½ way up.
10. Place in empty egg carton open side up. Set aside
11. Using a small juice cup, trace 12 circles (about 2-3 inch circle) onto tissue paper. Cut out 12 circles one for each egg.
12. Spread glue stick or paste over open edge of egg.
13. Place tissue circle over opening, turning down tissue edge on outside edge to cover hole.
14. Using markers or crayons, gently decorate egg shell.
15. Let dry before breaking.

THE CONFETTI QUILT

66" X 66"
DESIGNED AND CONSTRUCTED BY
JANE TENORIO-COSCARELLI
QUILTED BY DEBBIE JENKS

Confetti Egg Quilt Instructions
66" X 66"
All seams sewn with a 1/4" seam allowance

1/8 Yd.- Multicolored solids light to dark fabric
3/4 Yd.- Border one and three fabric
1 1/2 Yd.- Border two fabric
1 1/2 Yd.- Border four fabric
1/3 Yd.- Binding fabric
3 Yd.- Backing fabric
Miscellaneous fabric scraps for folk birds, flowers and eggs.
4- Medium buttons for eyes
70" X 70" Batting

Center

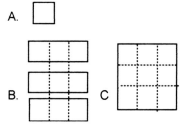

Cut 1- 3" strip from various multicolored fabric light to dark
Cut strips into 3" squares. You will need to cut 144 total A.
Lay them out to radiate light to dark, refer to quilt photo.
Once arranged, separate into rows. And then put into nine patch units B.
Sew 16 nine patches C. Sew 4 patches together to make 4 rows D.
Sew all 4 rows together to make 30 1/4" x 30 1/4" center. Press.

Border One

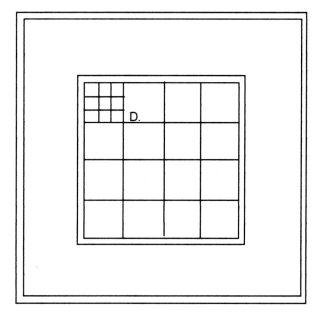

Cut 4-2" strips from border fabric. Cut 2 strips 30 1/4".
Sew to top and bottom of center. Press.
Cut 2 strips 33 1/4". Sew to sides of center. Press.

Border Two

Cut 2-10" strips from border two fabric.
Cut strips 33 1/4". Sew to side of center. Press.
Cut 3-10" strips. Sew together at each end,
making one strip. Fold strip in half.
Cut 2 strips 52". Sew to top and bottom of center.
Press.

Border Three

Cut 4 - 2" strips. Sew two together. Repeat.
Cut 2 strips 52".
Sew to top and bottom of center.
Cut 4 -2" Strips. Sew two together. Repeat.
Cut 2 strips 54 1/4". Sew to sides of center. Press.

Border Four

Cut 4 - 6" strips. Sew together to make two strips. Cut 2 strips 55 1/2". Sew to sides of center.
Cut 4 - 6" strips. Sew together to make two strips. Cut strips 66". Sew to top and bottom of center.

Appliqué Border

Trace all appliqué patterns remember to add seam allowance to appliqué templates. Refer to photo
placement. Baste or pin in position. Appliqué using method you prefer. Press.

Finishing

Layer top batting and backing. Baste in place. Hand or machine quilt. (Refer to basic quilt book
for directions if needed). Bind using any method you prefer.

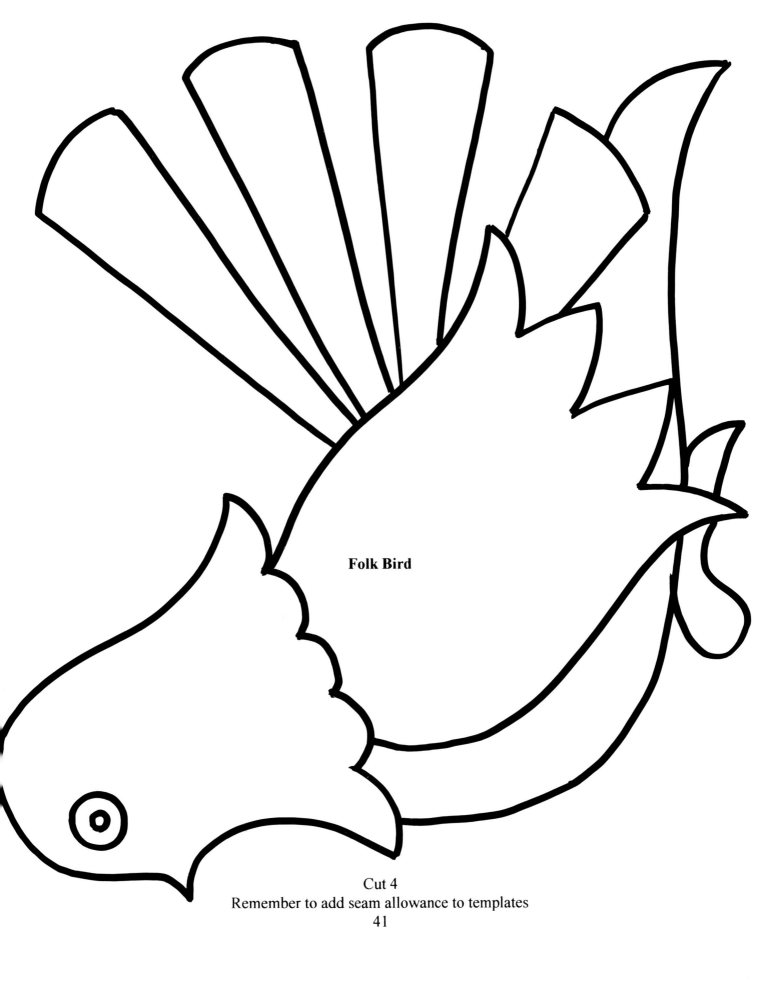

Folk Bird

Cut 4
Remember to add seam allowance to templates
41

Flower & Egg

Cut 4
Remember to add seam allowance to templates
43

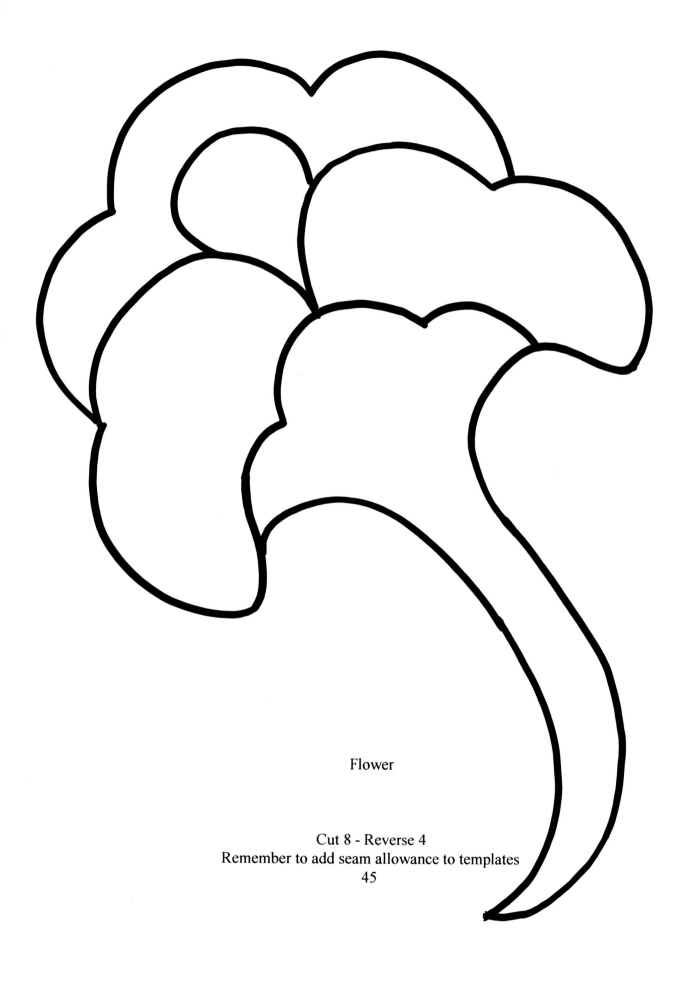

Flower

Cut 8 - Reverse 4
Remember to add seam allowance to templates
45

Other products from ¼ Inch Publishing

Books

The Tortilla Quilt
The Tamale Quilt
The Ants /Las Hormigas
The Piñata Quilt

Quilt Patterns

Coffee Girls	And Baby Makes Three	Raggedy Pals
Cat's Pajamas	Material Garden	Teas the Season
Deck the Cat	A Box of Chocolates	Heart of My Heart
Rodeo Stars	Roller Ghoster	Harvest Moon
Fall Friends	Winter Willie	Spring Seeds
Summer Picnic	Cooped Up	Mending Patches
Hen Pecked	Fiesta Red	Saucy Senorita
Precious Angels	Fairy Frolic	Oh Baby

Doll Patterns

Maria Doll   Quilt-a-beast Doll

**For author visits, lectures, workshop information
or to order contact:**

**¼ Inch Publishing
33255 Stoneman Street # B, Lake Elsinore Ca. 92530
Phone (909) 609-3309 Fax (909) 609-3369 Email Quarteri@aol.com
Visit our website www.quarterinchpublishing.com
or for catalog send a SASE**

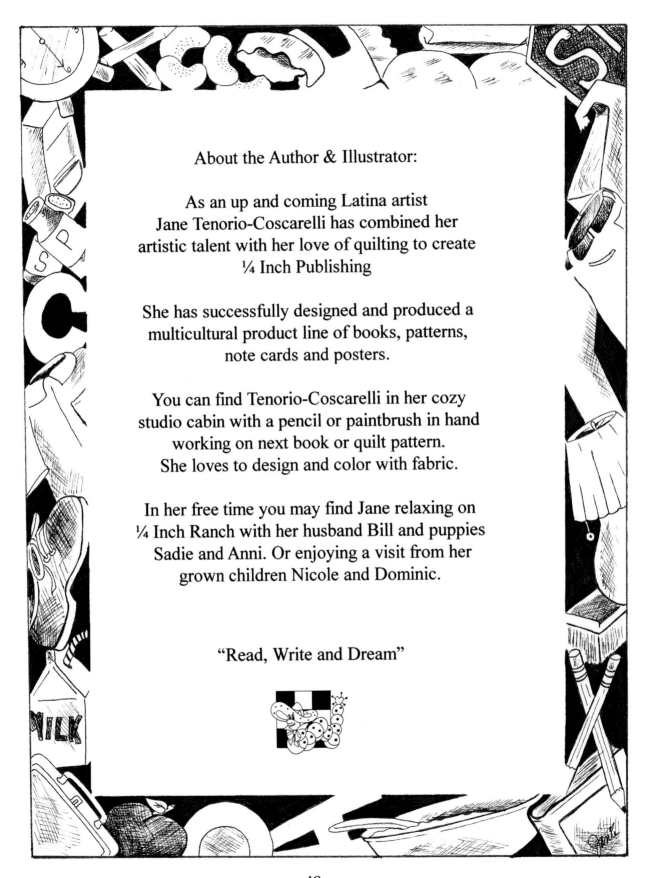

About the Author & Illustrator:

As an up and coming Latina artist
Jane Tenorio-Coscarelli has combined her
artistic talent with her love of quilting to create
¼ Inch Publishing

She has successfully designed and produced a
multicultural product line of books, patterns,
note cards and posters.

You can find Tenorio-Coscarelli in her cozy
studio cabin with a pencil or paintbrush in hand
working on next book or quilt pattern.
She loves to design and color with fabric.

In her free time you may find Jane relaxing on
¼ Inch Ranch with her husband Bill and puppies
Sadie and Anni. Or enjoying a visit from her
grown children Nicole and Dominic.

"Read, Write and Dream"